BUILDING WITH EARTH
Timeless Technique for Modern Architecture

© 2023 Instituto Monsa de ediciones.

First edition in September 2023 by Monsa Publications,
Carrer Gravina 43 (08930) Sant Adrià de Besós.
Barcelona (Spain)
T +34 933 810 093
www.monsa.com monsa@monsa.com

Editor and Project director Anna Minguet
Art director, layout and cover design
Eva Minguet (Monsa Publications)
Printed by Cachiman Grafic

Shop online:
www.monsashop.com

Follow us!
Instagram: @monsapublications

ISBN: 978-84-17557-70-6
B 16041-2023

BUILDING WITH EARTH

Timeless Technique for Modern Architecture

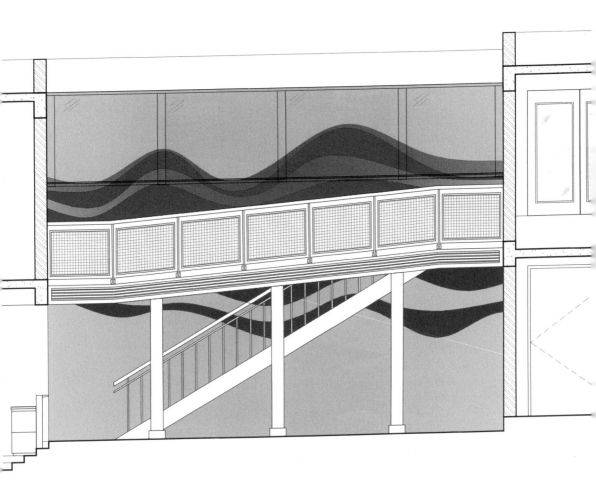

monsa

INTRO - Introducción

"Building with Earth" explores the beauty and versatility of rammed earth construction techniques. Through a compilation of 15 global projects, we showcase some of the finest architectural works utilizing this ancient method, ranging from modern designs to traditional buildings, with a strong focus on sustainability.

Rammed earth construction is an ancient technique used worldwide for centuries. Today, it has been revitalized as a sustainable, cost-effective building solution for the 21st century. In this book, architects present their projects through plans and photographs, allowing readers to explore how they have used this method to create aesthetically pleasing, sustainable structures that seamlessly integrate into the natural landscape.

"Building with Earth" explora la belleza y la versatilidad de la técnica de construcción de tierra apisonada, también conocida como "rammed earth". A través de la recopilación de 15 proyectos de todo el mundo, veremos algunos de los mejores trabajos de arquitectura que utilizan este milenario método, desde diseños modernos hasta edificaciones tradicionales, y todos ellos con un enfoque en la sostenibilidad.

La construcción de tierra apisonada es una técnica antigua que ha sido utilizada en todo el mundo durante siglos. Hoy en día, dicha técnica se ha revitalizado como una solución de construcción sostenible y de bajo costo para el siglo XXI. En este libro, los arquitectos presentan sus proyectos a través de planos y fotografías, donde gracias a sus explicaciones exploraremos cómo han utilizado este método para crear edificaciones hermosas y sostenibles que se integran armoniosamente en su entorno natural.

INDEX - Índice

MEETHI-MISHTI NU MATI GHAR

Sfera Blu Architects // Naman Shah
Ahmedabad, Gujarat, India // Photos © Umang Shah
www.namanshaharchitects.com
IG: @sferabluarchitects
IG: @naman2312
Facebook: @ blusphere5
Social Media Accounts: @sferabluarchitects
Contact: sferablu@gmail.com
Firm Location: Ahmedabad, Gujarat, India
Gross Built Area: 440 m2
Program: Residence for 2 children aged 3 & 9.
This house has a Parent Bedroom, Children Bedroom and a Guest
Bedroom. A large Living Room with a porch opening towards the
garden. Kitchen and Dining room. A Library, Secret Room and A Late
Night TV viewing Room. Supporting spaces such as Toilets and Stores.
Lead Architect: Naman Shah
Lead Architects e-mail: naman2312@gmail.com

Meethi and Mishti were clients, aged 3 and 9, respectively, and wanted an eco-friendly house that would not harm the nature around them. They suggested using minimal cement and bringing in less material from elsewhere, so the earth from the site was used to build the house through the rammed earth technology, which uses only 6-8 % of cement normally required for construction.

Different natural oxides were used to create layered fluid patterns on the walls, and the girls' stone and shell collections were added to preserve their fond memories. Upcycled wood from a demolished building was used to create frames, doors, and windows.

A dynamic ceiling made of sloping glass was designed to let diffused north light flow through the house, giving it a cool and airy feel. The house also included a playhouse with a slide, a secret room with three different entries, an acrobatic bed in the girls' room, and a bridge that ramps down to the girl's room for an impromptu catwalk. Blackboards were used as partitions, and a hidden basin was designed to address the girls' concern about seeing it while eating. Sketches from the girls' drawing books were used to create grills for the windows. The house embodies the people who live in it, and is both humane and honest.

Meethi y Mishti, clientes de 3 y 9 años, querían una casa ecológica que no dañara la naturaleza local. Propusieron usar el mínimo de cemento y traer menos materiales de otras partes, usando la tierra del lugar para construir la casa con tecnología de tierra apisonada, que solo usa el 6-8 % del cemento requerido normalmente.

Se usaron óxidos naturales para crear patrones en las paredes y las colecciones de piedras y conchas de las niñas se agregaron para preservar sus recuerdos. Se usaron materiales locales de bajo impacto ambiental y madera reutilizada para marcos, puertas y ventanas.

Un techo de vidrio inclinado deja pasar la luz difusa del norte, dándole una sensación fresca y aireada. También incluye una casita de juegos con tobogán, habitación secreta, cama acrobática y un puente que baja a la habitación de las niñas como una pasarela improvisada. Los bocetos de las niñas se usaron para crear rejillas para las ventanas. La casa encarna a las personas que viven en ella, siendo humana y honesta.

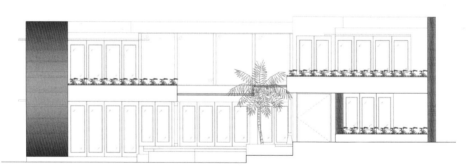

North elevation

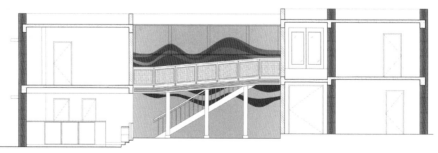

Section A-A'

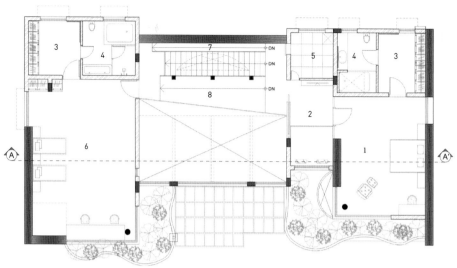

First floor plan

1. Master bedroom   5. Secret room
2. TV room   6. Daughter's room
3. Dressing   7. Slide
4. Toilet   8. Ramp

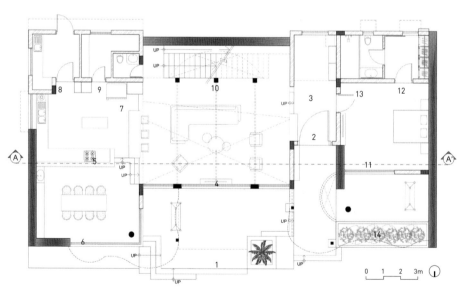

Ground floor plan

1. Patio   8. Utility
2. Entrance lobby   9. Store
3. Library   10. Slide
4. Living room   11. Guest bedroom
5. Kitchen   12. Dressing
6. Dining room   13. Toilet
7. Common toilet   14. Veranda

HOUSE AND EARTH & SKY

AIDLIN DARLING DESIGN // David Darling - Joshua Aidlin
Hillsborough, California, United States
Photos © Matthew Millman Photography
www.aidlindarlingdesign.com
Completion: June 2015
Size: 7,477 gross square feet,
5,609 conditioned square feet
Clients: Bay Chang & Sally Liu
General Contractor: Ryan Associates
Landscape Architect: Lutsko Associates
Structural Engineer: GFDS Engineers
Lighting Design: EJA Lighting Design
Geotechnical Engineer: Rollo & Ridley
Civil Engineer: Lea & Braze Engineering
Interior Design: Gary Hutton Design
Mechanical Engineer: Integral Group
Rammed Earth Consultant: Rammed Earth Works
LEED Consultant: Gilleran Energy Management
Specifications: White & Green Specs
Rainwater & Greywater Consultant: WaterSprout

This sustainable single-family home uses rammed earth walls and kite-like floating roofs to create indoor-outdoor living spaces that celebrate the intersection between earth and sky.

The extensive use of glass blurs the boundary between inside and outside, creating a natural garden-like environment. The owners set ambitious sustainability goals, striving for LEED Platinum certification and Net Zero Energy, and the design integrates ecological responsibility holistically.

The rammed earth walls provide thermal mass and bracket space, while the folded roof planes integrate multiple sustainable design strategies. The home is designed for Net Zero Energy and uses passive systems to address light and temperature, with electric-only mechanical systems providing balance. The goal is to create a sustainable building that endures, is beautiful and comfortable, and is a delight to live in for generations to come.

Esta casa unifamiliar sostenible utiliza muros de tierra compactada y techos flotantes en forma de cometa para crear espacios de vida interior-exterior que celebran la intersección entre la tierra y el cielo.

El uso extensivo de vidrio borra la frontera entre el interior y el exterior, creando un ambiente similar a un jardín natural. Los propietarios establecieron objetivos ambiciosos de sostenibilidad, luchando por la certificación LEED Platinum y Net Zero Energy, y el diseño integra la responsabilidad ecológica de manera global.

Los muros de tierra compactada proporcionan masa térmica y delimitan el espacio, mientras que los techos plegados integran múltiples estrategias de diseño sostenible. La casa está diseñada para Net Zero Energy y utiliza sistemas pasivos para abordar la luz y la temperatura, con sistemas mecánicos solo eléctricos que proporcionan equilibrio. El objetivo es crear un edificio sostenible que perdure, sea hermoso y cómodo, y que sea un placer vivir en él durante generaciones.

Render section

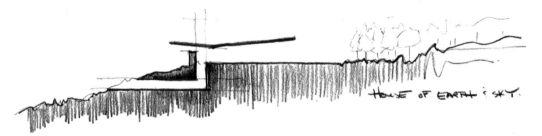

Sketch

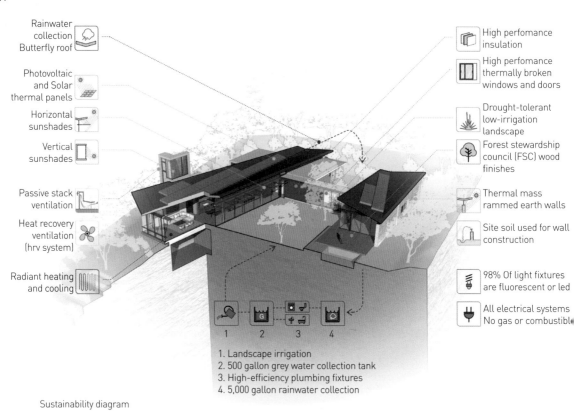

Rainwater collection Butterfly roof

Photovoltaic and Solar thermal panels

Horizontal sunshades

Vertical sunshades

Passive stack ventilation

Heat recovery ventilation (hrv system)

Radiant heating and cooling

High perfomance insulation

High perfomance thermally broken windows and doors

Drought-tolerant low-irrigation landscape

Forest stewardship council (FSC) wood finishes

Thermal mass rammed earth walls

Site soil used for wall construction

98% Of light fixtures are fluorescent or led

All electrical systems No gas or combustible

1   2   3   4

1. Landscape irrigation
2. 500 gallon grey water collection tank
3. High-efficiency plumbing fixtures
4. 5,000 gallon rainwater collection

Sustainability diagram

SONOMA RESIDENCE

ASQUARED STUDIOS // Jessie Whitesides, NCARB - Tony Garcia, AIA
Sonoma County, California, United States
Photos © adam potts photography, adampottsphotography.com
www.asquaredstudios.com
IG: @adampottsphoto
Design Architect: Asquared Studios, Jessie Whitesides, Ncarb, Architect Tony Garcia, AIA Architect
Client: Robert Mark Kamen
Landscape Architect: Roche + Roche
General Contractor: Annadel Builders, Inc.

Influenced by Japanese pagoda roof forms, this single-story vineyard residence uses a textural material palette of golden rammed earth, corten steel, renewable wood, and high-performing glass.

Designed to integrate itself into the rugged terrain, the design was developed as a series of interlocking boxes, arranged to maximize the views. The rammed earth walls frame windswept trees and seem to map the rows of grapevines renowned for making Kamen Estate Wines. Corten steel siding defines the structure's distinct forms.

A pagoda-style roof elevates the ceiling line above the expanses of window walls, opening the home to the land. Inside, the rammed earth is accentuated against neutral paint colors and accents of walnut, shou sugi ban, blackened steel, and concrete floors finished in a unique distressed finish.

This home is significant to the history of rammed earth construction in the United States, as it was the last true rammed earth home built by Rammed Earthworks and David Easton, the Grandfather of modern rammed earth construction.

Influenciada por las formas japonesas de los tejados de una pagoda, esta residencia de una sola planta en un viñedo utiliza una paleta de materiales texturizados de tierra apisonada dorada, acero corten, madera renovable y vidrio de alto rendimiento.

Diseñado para integrarse en el accidentado terreno, el diseño se desarrolló como una serie de cajas entrelazadas, dispuestas para maximizar las vistas. Los muros de tierra apisonada enmarcan árboles azotados por el viento y parecen trazar las hileras de vides famosas por la elaboración de los vinos Kamen Estate. El revestimiento de acero corten define las distintas formas de la estructura.

Un tejado en forma de pagoda eleva la línea del techo por encima de las grandes ventanas, abriendo la casa a la tierra. En el interior, la tierra apisonada se acentúa con colores neutros de pintura y detalles de nogal, shou sugi ban, acero ennegrecido y suelos de hormigón con un singular acabado envejecido.

Esta casa es importante para la historia de la construcción con tierra apisonada en los Estados Unidos, ya que fue la última verdadera casa de tierra apisonada construida por Rammed Earthworks y David Easton, el abuelo de la construcción moderna con tierra apisonada.

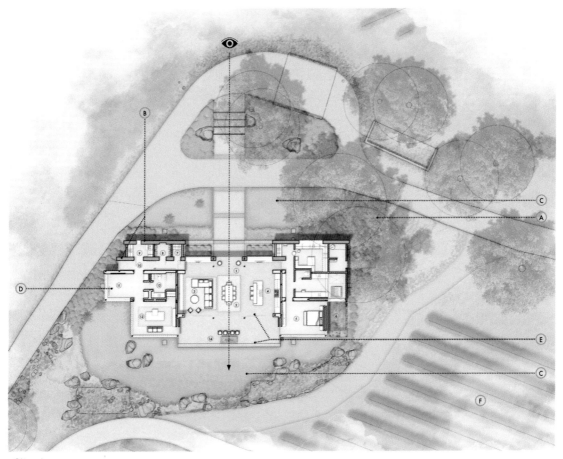

Site plan

Design axis: arrival progression + revealed view to San Francisco Bay

A. Heritage Oaks provide shade + support under-story growth attracting native pollinators
B. Exterior walls become interior finish with excellent thermal mass.
   Rammed Earth is a Low-carbon + Fire-resistant material
C. Native and drought tolerant landscaping surrounds the home bringing the outdoors - in
D. The house is composed of interlocking boxes designed to maximize daylighting and views
E. Sliding window wall opens to outdoor seating area, extending the interior living space outdoors
F. Estate vineyards

1. Entry
2. Dining
3. Living
4. Kitchen
5. Master wing
6. Zen garden
7. Closet
8. Wine library
9. Laundry
10. Gallery hall
11. Yoga room
12. Powder room
13. Office
14. Outdoor living

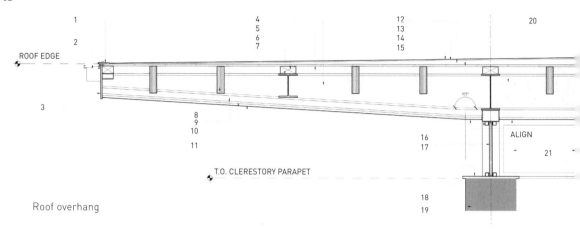

1 2 3 4 5 6 7 12 13 14 15 20

ROOF EDGE

177°

T.O. CLERESTORY PARAPET

8 9 10 11

16 17

ALIGN

21

18 19

Roof overhang

1. Durolast prefabricated drip edge with factory welded skirt and rectangular gutter.
2. Box gutter in corten finish to match nosing plate
3. 1/2" x 12" steel nosing plate, corten finish
4. Structural steel girder beyond, s.S.D.
5. 2 1/2" Closed cell spray foam insulation to fill nailer space
6. 3x nailer typical, S.S.D.
7. Structural steel framing, S.S.D.
8. LVL framing, S.S.D., typical
9. Provide furring to dropped wood ceiling
10. 5/8" type 'x' dry wall as backing to wood ceiling finish
11. 1x8 wood plank ceiling, made from 1 x 10 board with 1.25" Shiplap joint. See finish schedule for additional information. Joint to be set tight see rcp for board layout

12. 5/8" Plywood shear, s.S.D.
13. Sloped rigid insulation, 1/8" per ft.
14. 1/4" Densdeck roofing board
15. Class 'a' roofing: 50 mil. Durolast membrane
16. HSS 6" x 4" as top chord of vierendeel truss, s.S.D.
17. Clerestory window
18. 4" Steel plate as bottom chord of vierendeel truss, s.S.D.
19. Rammed earth wall
20. Provide R30 batt insulation at interior
21. Clerestory window at side wall

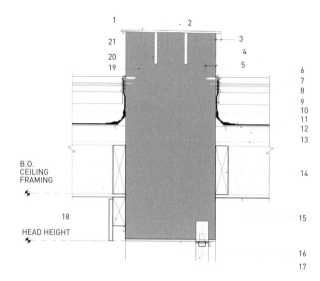

Parapet detail

1. 3/8" Corten steel plate
2. Slope down 1/8" per ft
3. 1" Each side
4. Duro-last chaulk
5. Stainless steel counter-flashing fastened 6-inches on center with duro-last fastener. Let-in to rammed earth wall
6. Duro-last membrane must extend 3/4-inch beyond fastener
7. Duro-last sealant
8. Duro-last prefabricated parapet wall flashing
9. Durolast cant strip
10. Durolast 50mil roofing
11. 1/4" Dens deck roof board
12. Sloped foam panel
13. Roof sheathing, s.S.D.
14. Roof framing and insulation per plans, s.S.D.
15. Gyp. Board finish per plans
16. See door detail at this location for additional information
17. Door per schedule
18. 3/4" x 8" wood
Trim and picture rail, typ.
19. Rammed earth wall per plan
20. 5/8" x 6" steel dowels welded to plate at 24" o.C. (Staggered)
21. 1/8" Radius drip edge

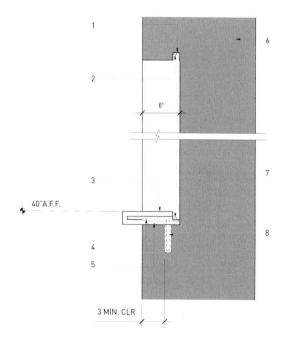

Nitch Detail

1. 1 1/4" x 1 1/4" x 1/8" aluminum u-channel embedded into rammed earth at head and jambs of niche, paint channel black
2. Led strip light cont. around niche set into aluminum channel
3. Solid surface niche shelf, miter corners typical
4. 1/2" P.T. Plywood
5. 3/4" P.T. Plywood
6. Rammed earth wall
7. Mount lighting on plywood shelf support at sill. Paint plywood black
8. Drill and epoxy attachment for shelf to rammed earth

CASA TIERRA

AAE | arquitectura // Arturo Aguilar Espinoza - Javier Díaz Cerón
Ciudad de México, Mexico // Photos © Javier Díaz
www.aaearquitectura.com
Design Architects: Arturo Aguilar Espinoza, Javier Díaz Cerón
Client: Private
Client Project Managers: AAE arquitectura
Centre: Bosque Real, México
The Collaborative Artwork by: Raíz Arquitectura, Karen Poulain,
Gabriela Amicone
Landscape Architect: AAE arquitectura
Civil Engineer: Juan Marcos Hernández Horroa

This house uses a biophilic concept that focuses on the use of natural materials, especially earth, to build hierarchical walls both inside and outside the house. Circulations are designed to highlight architectural elements and are accompanied by natural ones.

From the rooftop, views of the city are enjoyed, and social spaces are created with gardens and orchards. The house has a double-height study-library, as well as intimate spaces with views of garden areas or city landscapes.

Casa Tierra is part of a pair of houses that share a central garden for coexistence, but maintain the privacy of each one. Located in an exclusive subdivision in Mexico City, this house is a great investment to live in an architectural and natural space that promotes the use of natural materials with a low carbon footprint and timeless design.

Esta casa utiliza un concepto biofílico que se enfoca en el uso de materiales naturales, especialmente la tierra, para construir muros jerárquicos en el interior y exterior de la casa. Las circulaciones se diseñan para resaltar los elementos arquitectónicos y están acompañadas por elementos naturales.

Desde la azotea, se puede disfrutar de vistas hacia la ciudad y se crean espacios sociales con jardines y huertos. La casa tiene un estudio-biblioteca de doble altura, así como espacios íntimos con vistas hacia áreas ajardinadas o paisajes de la ciudad.

La Casa Tierra forma parte de un par de viviendas que comparten un jardín central para la convivencia, pero mantienen la privacidad de cada una. Ubicada en un fraccionamiento exclusivo de la Ciudad de México, esta casa es una gran inversión para vivir en un espacio arquitectónico y natural, que promueve el uso de materiales naturales con baja huella de carbono y con un diseño atemporal.

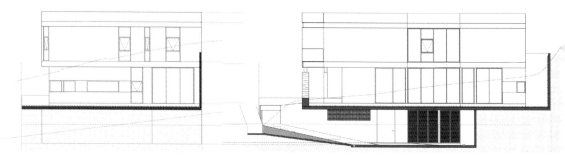

North elevation

East elevation

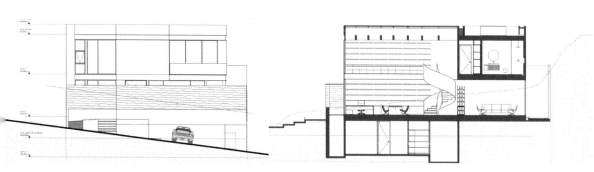

South elevation

A-A' section

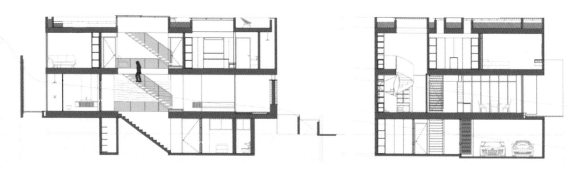

B-B' section

C-C' section

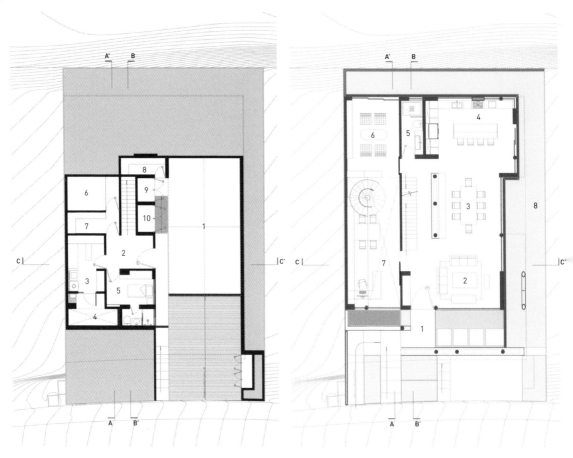

Basement plan

1. Garage
2. Hall
3. Laundry
4. Patio
5. Maiden room
6. Mechanical room
7. Cellar
8. Store
9. Boilers
10. Trash

First level plan

1. Hall
2. Living room
3. Dining room
4. Kitchen
5. Guest bathroom
6. Chess room
7. Office
8. Garden

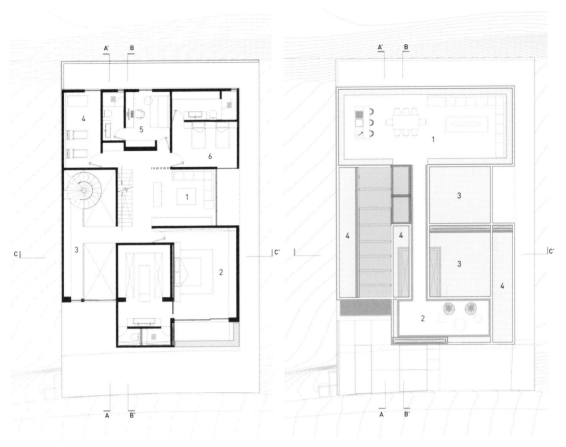

Second level plan

1. Family room
2. Master bedroom
3. Library
4. Gym
5. Study
6. Bedroom

Rooftop plan

1. Terrace
2. Lookout
3. Orchard
4. Garden

ESPACIO KAAB

Di Frenna Arquitectos // Matia Di Frenna Müller
Nogueras, Comala, Colima, México // Photos © Lorena Darquea
www.difrennaarquitectos.com
Area: 401.00 m²
Work Team: Arch. Matia Di Frenna Müller,
Arch. Mariana de la Mora Padilla,
Ing. Juan Gerardo Guardado Ávila
Project Type: Single Family Residential

Alejandro Rangel Hidalgo, known for his skill in the arts and crafts of Colima, lived in the Nogueras estate for many years. The Espacio Kaab project honors this site and the artisan's craft. The area is a unique ecosystem, with dry vegetation, cacti, stones, and earth.

The house adapts to the terrain with a modular architectural program while respecting the topography. The main concept is the integration of indoor and outdoor spaces, using materials originating from Comala such as rammed earth walls and palm trees. The house has retaining walls that provide nooks and contemplation spaces.

The intention is to generate open spaces with perspectives from inside the building. The interior design uses stone and wood furniture in its purest state, with indirect and highlighted lighting. Espacio Kaab is the latest addition to the Nogueras estate.

Alejandro Rangel Hidalgo, conocido por su habilidad en el arte y artesanías de Colima, vivió en la Hacienda de Nogueras por muchos años. El proyecto Espacio Kaab honra este recinto y el oficio del artesano. La zona es un ecosistema único, con vegetación seca, árida, cactus, piedras y tierra.

La casa se adapta al terreno con un programa arquitectónico modular, respetando la topografía. El concepto principal es la integración de los espacios interiores y exteriores, utilizando materiales originarios de Comala como muros de tapial y palma. La casa cuenta con muros de contención que dotan de recovecos y espacios de contemplación.

La intención es generar espacios abiertos con perspectivas desde el interior de la construcción. El diseño interior utiliza muebles de piedra y madera en su estado más puro, con iluminación indirecta y destacada. Espacio Kaab es la más reciente adición a la hacienda de Nogueras.

Front elevation

Lateral elevation

Rear elevation

Lateral elevation

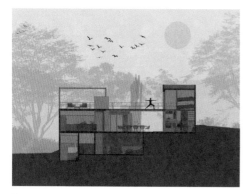

Section

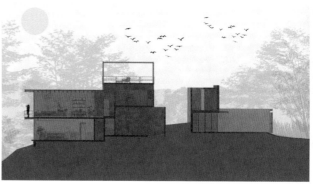

Section

WITKLIPFONTEIN ECO LODGE

GLH ARCHITECTS // Xavier Huyberechts - Damien Huyberechts
Vredefort, Free State, South Africa // Photos © Elsa Young
www.witklipfontein.co.za - www.glh.co.za
Architects: Xavier Huyberechts & Damien Huyberechts,
GLH Architects
Consultants:
- Quantity Surveying: Xavier Huyberechts, GLH Architects
- Project Manager: Damien Huyberechts
- Civil Engineering: Craig Thompson, PURE Engineers
- Mechanical Engineering: Xavier Huyberechts, GLH Architects
- Principal Contractor: Damien Huyberechts
- Electrical Engineering: Damien Huyberechts
- Landscape: Xavier Huyberechts, GLH Architects and
Damien Huyberechts
- Green/Sustainable Consultants: Xavier Huyberechts, GLH Archi-
  tects and Damien Huyberechts
Client: Xavier Huyberechts and Carine Huyberechts - Bwakira
Contractors: Damien Huyberechts, main contractor
Timeline: 2016-2018
Area: 400 m2

The lodge is an architecturally unique building that seamlessly integrates into its natural surroundings through the use of traditional vernacular building techniques and modern minimalistic design.

Its aim is to rethink the concept of a house/lodge by utilizing eco-friendly practices and technologies that are respectful to the environment. Overlooking the plains, the lodge uses the principle of thermal mass to flatten temperatures throughout the year, avoiding mechanical air conditioning.

It also features a range of sustainable innovations, such as cement-free construction, recycled granite floors, and solar water heating.

Overall, the lodge serves as a testament to the idea that traditional building techniques, such as rammed earth, can be reinterpreted in a modern way to create innovative and environmentally friendly architecture.

El lodge es un edificio arquitectónicamente único que se integra perfectamente en su entorno natural mediante el uso de técnicas de construcción vernáculas tradicionales y un diseño minimalista moderno.

Su objetivo es repensar el concepto de casa/lodge utilizando prácticas y tecnologías ecológicas que sean respetuosas con el medio ambiente. Con vistas a las llanuras, el lodge utiliza el principio de la masa térmica para aplanar las temperaturas durante todo el año evitando el aire acondicionado mecánico.

También cuenta con una gama de innovaciones sostenibles, como la construcción sin cemento, pisos de granito reciclado y calefacción solar de agua.

En general, el lodge sirve como un testimonio de que las técnicas de construcción tradicionales como la tierra compactada pueden reinterpretarse de manera moderna para crear una arquitectura innovadora y respetuosa con el medio ambiente.

Elevations

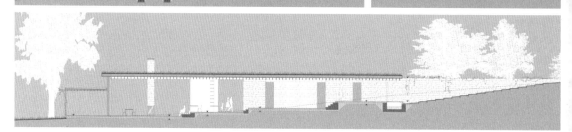

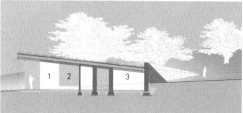

Sections

1. Bedroom	5. Back of kitchen	9. Living room
2. Bathroom	6. Technical room	10. Dining room
3. Store	7. Maid room	11. Drain water tank
4. Kitchen	8. Kids bedroom	

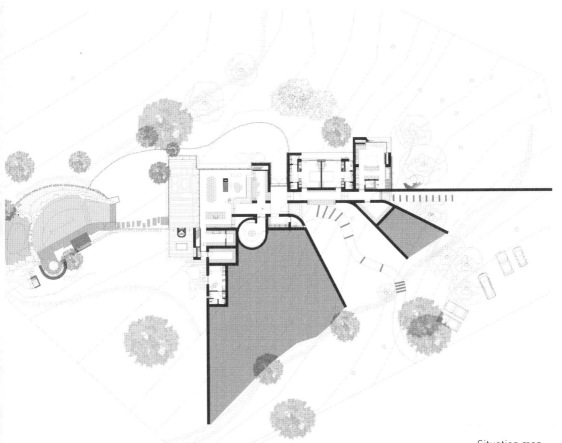

Situation map

CASA MARTHA

Nativa Arquitectura // Alfredo Navarro Tiznado
La Misión, Baja California, Mexico // Photos © Oscar Hernández
IG: @arquitectura.nativa
Architect: Alfredo Navarro Tiznado
Design Team: Kenia Esmeralda García Rosas, and
Hanna Appel Hernández
Construction: Pedro Luis Curiel Bojórquez,
José Francisco Ramírez García

Casa Martha is an archaeologist's home designed with rudimental and artisanal techniques, unifying time, form, and context through composition and materiality of ancestral origin. Located in the urban area of La Misión, between Ensenada and Rosarito, the lot has dimensions of 15 x 40 meters on rugged topography.

The program includes a retirement home for a couple, Martha and Bill, and a space for plastic arts. The house is blended with the site, and a dialogue is created between three volumes embedded in the site, oriented towards the Pacific Ocean.

The first level has two areas, the visitor area, and the study area.

The second level has the entertainment room, dining room, and kitchen, accessed through large windows and porches woven with salt pine.

At the back of the social area, a staircase leads to the third level, where the main chamber is located.

Casa Martha is modeled with deep sensitivity and respect for its surroundings, using compacted earth as the main construction element.

Casa Martha es la casa de un arqueólogo diseñada con técnicas rudimentarias y artesanales, unificando el tiempo, la forma y el contexto a través de la composición y la materialidad de origen ancestral. Ubicada en el área urbana de La Misión, entre Ensenada y Rosarito, el lote tiene dimensiones de 15 x 40 metros en una topografía accidentada.

El programa incluye una casa de retiro para una pareja, Martha y Bill, y un espacio para artes plásticas. La casa se integra con el sitio, y se crea un diálogo entre tres volúmenes incrustados en el sitio, orientados hacia el Océano Pacífico.

El primer nivel tiene dos áreas, el área de visitantes y el área de estudio.

El segundo nivel tiene la sala de entretenimiento, comedor y cocina, accesibles a través de grandes ventanales y porches tejidos con pino salado.

En la parte trasera del área social, una escalera conduce al tercer nivel, donde se encuentra la cámara principal.

Casa Martha está modelada con profunda sensibilidad y respeto por su entorno, utilizando tierra compactada como el elemento principal de construcción.

Longitudinal section

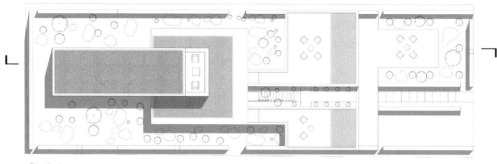

Roof plan

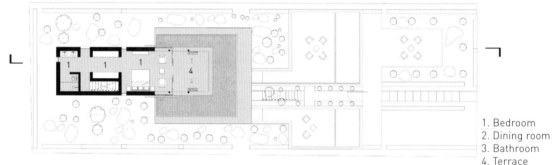

Third level plan

1. Bedroom
2. Dining room
3. Bathroom
4. Terrace

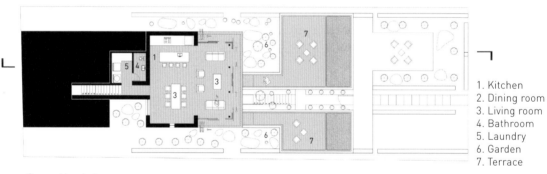

Second level plan

1. Kitchen
2. Dining room
3. Living room
4. Bathroom
5. Laundry
6. Garden
7. Terrace

First level plan

1. Parking
2. Kitchen
3. Bedroom
4. Bathroom
5. Storage
6. Garden
7. Terrace

0 1 2   5 m

HERDADE DA CARDEIRA

Embaixada // Cristina Mendonça - Nuno Griff e Paulo Goinhas
Orada, Borba, Portugal // Photos © Simone Bossi
www.embaixada.net
Client: Herdade da Cardeira,
Erika & Thomas Meier
Landscape Architect: Sandra Nunes
Civil Engineer: Pedro Fragoso Viegas
Rammed Earth Consulting: Henrique Schreck
Building Contractor: Construções Monsaraz

This project consisted of the extension of an existing winery at Herdade da Cardeira in Borba, Portugal. A house and office area were designed to support the winery's activities and the aim was to integrate the existing buildings with the new construction.

The strategy involved flattening the terrain and placing the new buildings at different levels along the hill to accommodate the privacy needs of each use. Local materials and cross-ventilation techniques were used to improve energy efficiency.

The project took eight years to complete and focused on seamless integration between indoor and outdoor spaces, and between residential and winery areas. The property is conceived as a single entity where agriculture, commerce and housing share space.

Este proyecto consistió en la expansión de una bodega existente en la Herdade da Cardeira en Borba, Portugal. Se diseñó una casa y una zona de oficinas para apoyar la actividad de la bodega y se buscó integrar las construcciones preexistentes con la nueva edificación.

La estrategia consistió en suavizar la topografía del terreno y ubicar las nuevas construcciones en diferentes niveles a lo largo de la colina, para adaptarse a las necesidades de privacidad de cada uso. Se utilizaron materiales locales y técnicas de ventilación cruzada para mejorar la eficiencia energética.

El proyecto tomó ocho años para completarse y se enfocó en una integración fluida entre los espacios interiores y exteriores, y entre las áreas residenciales y de la bodega. La propiedad se concibe como una sola entidad donde la agricultura, el comercio y la vivienda comparten espacio.

Site plan

A. Entrance gate
B. Wine cellar (pre-existent)
C. Wine cellar support area
D. Housing area (social)
E. Housing (bedrooms)
F. Parking
G. Power and water supply house | recycling waste

1. Entrance path
2. Refreshment pergola
3. Olive grove terrace
4. Vine terrace
5. "Monte" hill
6. Vine path
7. Olive grove path
8. Pool terrace
9. White wisterias path

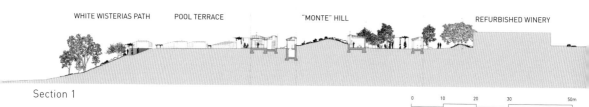

WHITE WISTERIAS PATH   POOL TERRACE   "MONTE" HILL   REFURBISHED WINERY

Section 1

0   10   20   30   50m

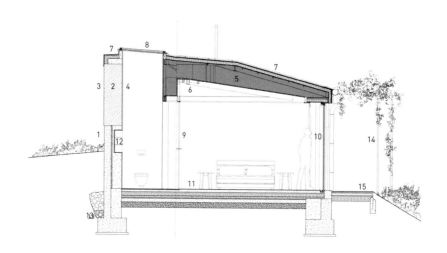

1. Structural concrete
2. Rammed earth
3. Lime plaster, refined to the colour of the rammed earth
4. Lime plaster, white colour
5. Light steel frame
6. Structure in solid pine wood
7. Covering system in natural zinc
8. Roof window in anodised aluminium, gray colour
9. Solid door in riga wood (reused)
10. Sliding door in anodised aluminium, light champagne colour
11. Flooring in polished concrete
12. Hidraulic mosaic
13. Drainage system
14. Pergola in steel, dark grey colour
15. Stabilised gravel with corten steel

Housing area (social) plan

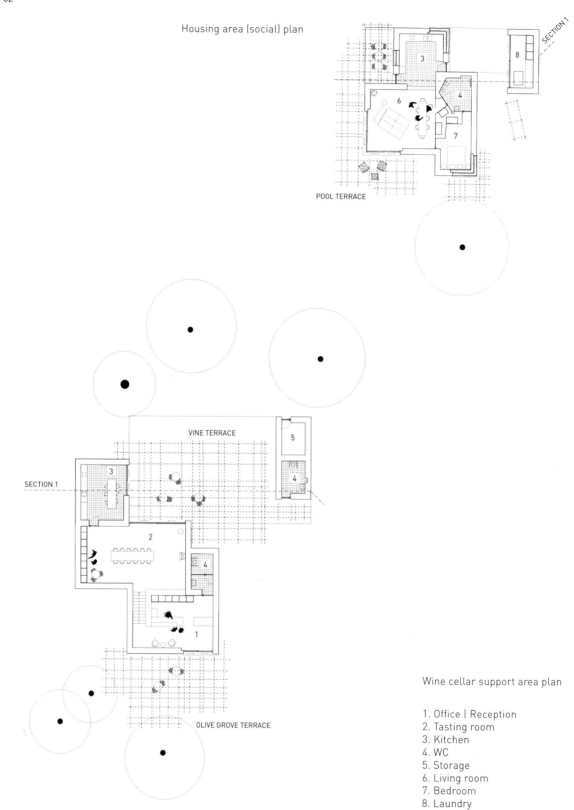

POOL TERRACE

VINE TERRACE

SECTION 1

OLIVE GROVE TERRACE

Wine cellar support area plan

1. Office | Reception
2. Tasting room
3. Kitchen
4. WC
5. Storage
6. Living room
7. Bedroom
8. Laundry

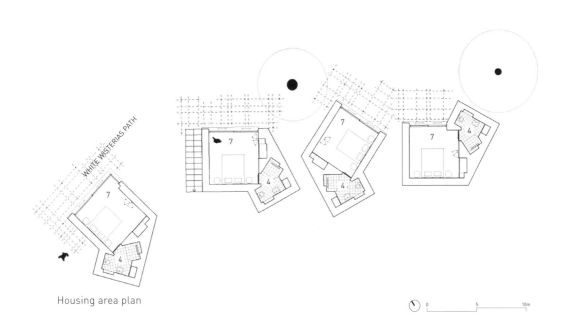

WHITE WISTERIAS PATH

Housing area plan

0   5   10m

CANYON ROAD BRIDGE HOUSE

Arkin Tilt Architects
Santa Fe, New Mexico, United States // Photos © Kate Russell
www.arkintilt.com
Design Architect: David Arkin, AIA
Design Project Manager: Devin Kinney
Client: Julie Stachowiak and Tuck Stibich
Contractor: Prull Custom Builders of Santa Fe
Drawings by: Arkin Tilt Architects
Landscape Architect: Donna Bone/Design with Nature
Civil Engineer: Morey Walker

This house in Santa Fe's historic district is located on a rolling wooded site, the dining room bridges a dry arroyo to access the living space which enjoys views of downtown Santa Fe.

The house combines traditional construction elements with modern high-performance systems and richly textured materials. The living room features ICF walls with lime plaster, concrete floors, and a rammed earth masonry fireplace wall that adds thermal mass and improves the home's passive solar performance. Salvaged wood and locally harvested spruce are used for interior accents.

Access to the house is through a covered courtyard with an outdoor rammed earth "kiva" - a take on the traditional Santa Fe fireplace. Sean Kaltenbach of New Mexico Earthworks led the construction of the rammed earth features.

Esta casa en el distrito histórico de Santa Fe está ubicada en un terreno boscoso ondulado, el comedor conecta un arroyo seco para acceder al espacio habitable que goza de vistas del centro de Santa Fe.

La casa combina elementos de construcción tradicionales con sistemas modernos de alto rendimiento y materiales texturizados de alta calidad. La sala de estar presenta paredes de ICF con yeso de cal, pisos de concreto y una pared de chimenea de albañilería de tierra apisonada que agrega masa térmica y mejora el rendimiento solar pasivo de la casa. Se utilizan madera recuperada y abeto cosechado localmente para los acentos interiores.

El acceso a la casa es a través de un patio cubierto con una «kiva» de tierra apisonada al aire libre, una versión de la tradicional chimenea de Santa Fe. Sean Kaltenbach de New Mexico Earthworks lideró la construcción de las características de tierra apisonada.

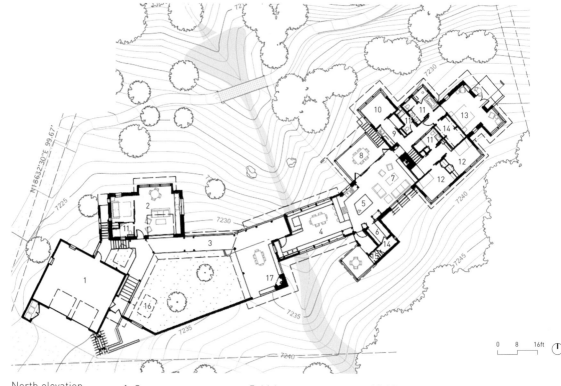

North elevation

1. Garage
2. Casita-guest house
3. Covered walkway
4. Dining & entry bridge
5. Kitchen
6. Pantry

7. Living
8. Cantilevered deck
9. Laundry
10. Art studio
11. Bathroom
12. Bedroom

13. Master bedroom
14. Closet/storage
15. Stairs to roof
16. Stormwater cistern
17. KIVA

AIREYS HOUSE

Studio Nicholas Burns // Nicholas Burns
Victoria, Australia // Photos © Peter Bennetts
www.nicholas-burns.com
Design Architect: Nicholas Burns
Client Project Managers: N.A.
The Collaborative Artwork by: N.A.
Landscape Architect: N.A.
Civil Engineer: Engineering Elements, Melbourne

The house in Aireys Inlet, Australia is located on a wooded site and has views of the ocean, lighthouse, and valley. The design of the house fits the site and existing vegetation, with rammed earth walls framing the view and connecting the experience to nature.

The east-west orientation allows winter sun to penetrate the living areas and cool southern breezes to flow in from the ocean. Framed windows and openings allow for natural ventilation and cross-flow of air, while intimate niches provide views for quiet reflection.

The bedrooms are protected yet offer panoramic views of the landscape. The design is attuned to the rhythms of nature and the environment, seeking a deep connection with nature.

La casa en Aireys Inlet, Australia, está ubicada en un terreno boscoso y cuenta con vistas al océano, al faro y al valle. El diseño de la casa se ajusta al sitio y la vegetación existente, con muros de tierra apisonada que enmarcan la vista y conectan la experiencia con la naturaleza.

La orientación este-oeste permite que el sol de invierno penetre en las áreas de estar y que las brisas frescas del sur lleguen desde el océano. Las ventanas enmarcadas y las aberturas permiten la ventilación natural y el flujo de aire cruzado, mientras que los nichos íntimos ofrecen vistas para la reflexión tranquila.

Las habitaciones están protegidas y, al mismo tiempo, proporcionan una vista panorámica del paisaje. El diseño se ajusta a los ritmos de la naturaleza y el entorno, y busca una conexión profunda con la naturaleza.

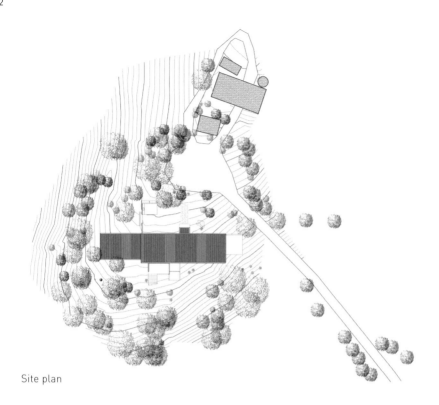

Site plan

North elevation

South elevation

East elevation

West elevation

JULIMAR FALLS HOUSE

Studio Nicholas Burns // Nicholas Burns
Perth, Australia // Photos © Peter Bennetts
www.nicholas-burns.com
Design Architect: Nicholas Burns
Client Project Managers: N.A.
The Collaborative Artwork by: N.A.
Landscape Architect: N.A.
Civil Engineer: Roger Pateman
Materials: rammed earth walls, concrete screed floors,
steel / galvanised iron roof, stone - solid carved basins and bath,
marri timber

Located in the Chittering valley, one and a half hours north of Perth, the landscape is a mix of cleared farming areas and bushland. The house is nestled into a steeply sloped hill, creating a refuge and a frame for connecting occupants to the environment.

The design provides a series of interrelated experiences using low maintenance, weathering materials, leaving an unfinished look that integrates with the landscape.

Open living spaces connect with courtyards and decking areas, framing nature and providing contrasting outdoor spaces for sitting and eating. Rammed earth walls provide thermal mass, and high-performance glazing, ventilation, and geothermal convective systems maintain comfort with low energy consumption.

The house serves as a private retreat for the owners and a meeting place for extended family, with a courtyard garden in raised corten beds for producing fruit, herbs, and vegetables. Museum-grade LED lighting displays art to its best and provides essential quality without natural light.

Ubicada en el valle de Chittering, a una hora y media al norte de Perth, el paisaje es una mezcla de áreas de cultivo y bosques. La casa está ubicada en una ladera empinada, creando un refugio y un marco para conectar a los ocupantes con el entorno.

El diseño ofrece una serie de experiencias interrelacionadas utilizando materiales de bajo mantenimiento y envejecidos, dejando un aspecto sin acabado que se integra con el paisaje.

Los espacios de vida abiertos se conectan con patios y áreas de cubierta, enmarcando la naturaleza y proporcionando espacios al aire libre contrastantes para sentarse y comer. Las paredes de tierra apisonada proporcionan masa térmica, y los vidrios de alto rendimiento, la ventilación y los sistemas convectivos geotérmicos mantienen el confort con un bajo consumo de energía.

La casa sirve como un retiro privado para los propietarios y un lugar de reunión para la familia extendida, con un jardín interior en camas elevadas de acero corten para producir frutas, hierbas y verduras. La iluminación LED de calidad de museo muestra el arte de la mejor manera posible y proporciona una calidad esencial sin luz natural.

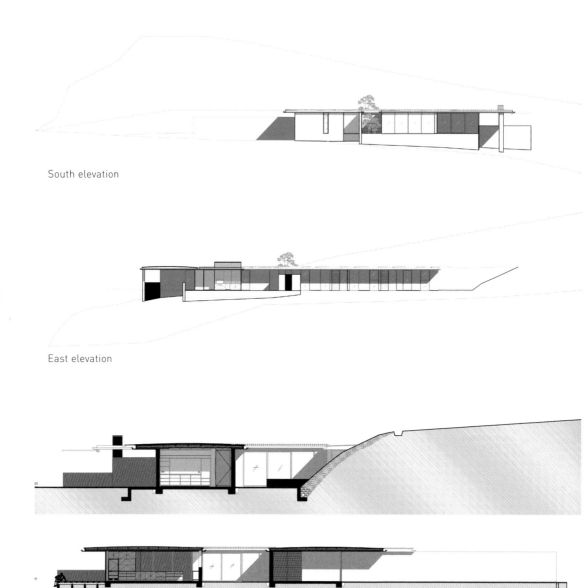

South elevation

East elevation

Section A

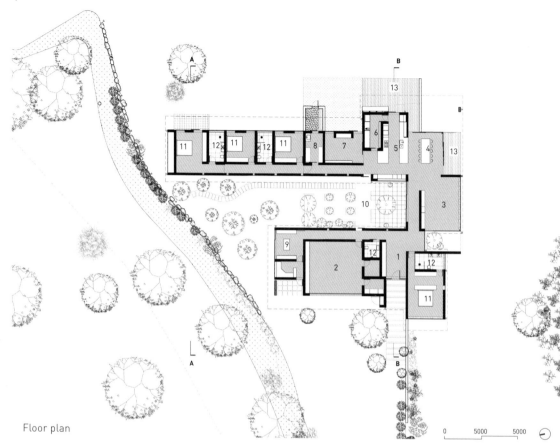

Floor plan

1. Entrance
2. Garage
3. Living room
4. Dining room
5. Kitchen
6. Pantry
7. Games room
8. Laundry
9. Office
10. Court
11. Room
12. Bathroom
13. Terrace

0   5000   5000

PERICOS

Lucila Aguilar Arquitectos // Lucila Aguilar
Soconusco region, Chiapas, Mexico
Photos © Lucila Aguilar de la Lama
www.lucilaaguilar.com
Design Architect: Lucila Aguilar Arquitectos
Client: Finca Don Jorge
Principal in Charge: Lucila Aguilar de la Lama
Bamboo Constructor: Bolivar Epigmenio Garcia Miranda
Design Team: Miguel Ruiz Velasco, Habid Athie,
Ricardo Romero, Paola Calzada
Administration: María Teresa Moreno
Civil Engineer: Cesar Moreno Peralta

Finca Don Jorge is located in Mexico Soconusco Region, in a state-of-the-art 110-hectare cacao plantation.

The compound consists of 5 modules with 9 rooms that have an impressive view of the Tacaná volcano. The sustainable design leverages from the natural materials available in the area: Earth, Bamboo, Wood, River Rocks.

The adobe walls are separated from the humidity of the ground with river stone. The bamboo and esterilla roof is covered in vegetation to maintain a cool temperature.

The "Pericos" rooms blend in with nature and visitors can enjoy the birds songs and the peaceful atmosphere while reconnecting with Mexican cacao and it´s ancient legacy.

La Finca Don Jorge, ubicada en la Región Soconusco de México, dentro de una plantación de 110 hectáreas de cacao de última generación.

El conjunto consta de 5 módulos con 9 habitaciones que disfrutan de una impresionante vista del volcán Tacaná. El diseño sustentable se pensó para aprovechar los materiales naturales disponibles en la zona: Tierra, Bambú, Madera, Piedra Bola.

Sus muros de adobe están protegidos de la humedad del suelo con piedras de río. El techo de bambú y esterilla está cubierto de vegetación para mantener una temperatura fresca.

Las habitaciones «Pericos» se integran con el paisaje para que los huéspedes pueden disfrutar del canto de las aves y la paz del ambiente, mientras se reconectan con el cacao mexicano, un gran legado ancestral.

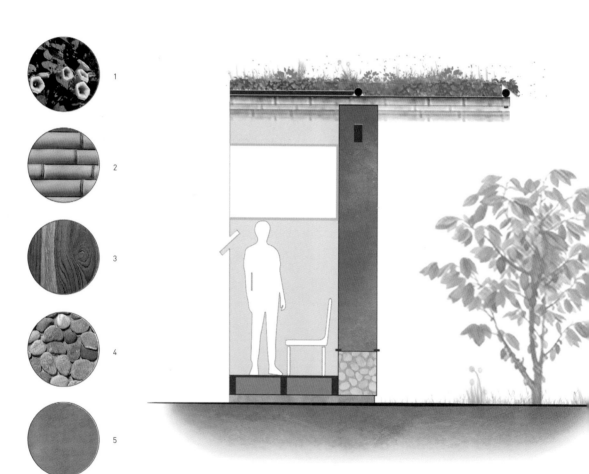

Constructive section

1. Vegetation Insulating cover
2. Bamboo Structure
3. Wood Floors
4. Stone Superbasement
5. Earth Adobes

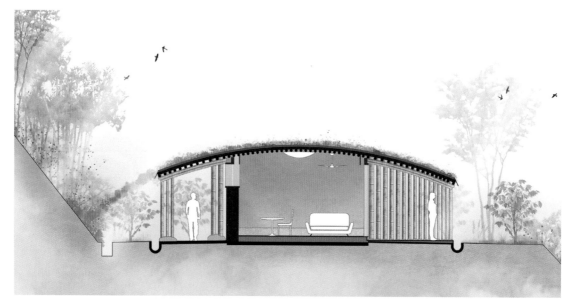

General section

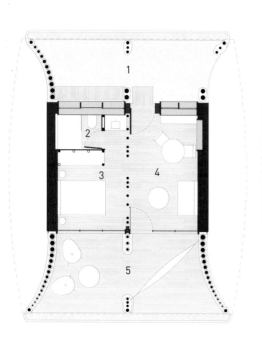

Suite module. Floor plan

Bedroom module. Floor plan

1. Access portico
2. Bathroom
3. Bedroom
4. Living area
5. Terrace

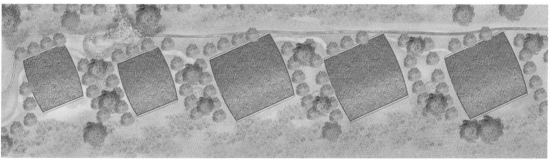

Site plan

TK PAD

Ward | Blake Architects // Tom Ward - Mitch Blake
Jackson, Wyoming, United States // Photos © Paul Warchol
www.wardblake.com
Design Architect: Thomas Ward, AIA
Client: Katherine Reedy
Client Project Managers: Stephen Kaness
Landscape Architect: N/A
Civil Engineer: Niskian Monks Engineers Ty Monks, PE

The site features wind-blown Loess fill from the Caldera of Yellowstone National Park and a unique outcrop of Conglomerate, remnants of a prehistoric inland sea.

These geological features informed the design of the Residence, which is oriented along an east-west axis to face south.

Wood-framed walls divide public and private spaces, and rammed earth walls utilize a patented post-tensioning steel system.

Native soil and crusher fines are joined with Portland cement to form the walls, which offer passive thermal resistance and acoustic properties.

The house envelope features elemental materials, including untreated concrete and native wood treated with water-borne sealers.

El sitio cuenta con sedimentos de loess transportados por el viento desde la Caldera del Parque Nacional Yellowstone y una singular formación rocosa de conglomerado, restos de un antiguo mar interior.

Estas características geológicas influyeron en el diseño de la residencia, que se orienta a lo largo de un eje este-oeste para enfrentar al sur.

Las paredes con estructura de madera dividen los espacios públicos y privados, mientras que las paredes de tierra compactada utilizan un sistema patentado de tensión de acero.

El suelo nativo y los residuos de trituración se unen con cemento Portland para formar las paredes, que ofrecen resistencia térmica pasiva y propiedades acústicas.

El revestimiento de la casa utiliza materiales elementales, incluyendo hormigón sin tratar y madera autóctona tratada con selladores a base de agua.

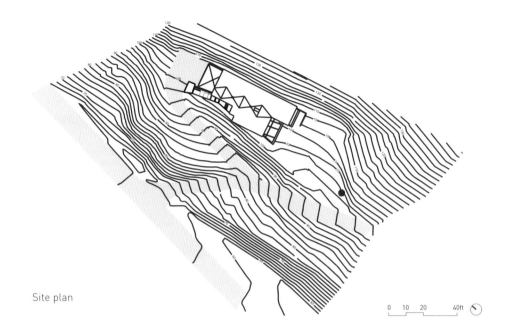

Site plan

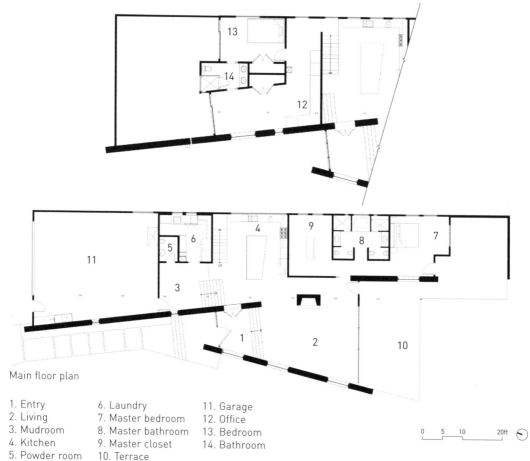

Main floor plan

1. Entry
2. Living
3. Mudroom
4. Kitchen
5. Powder room
6. Laundry
7. Master bedroom
8. Master bathroom
9. Master closet
10. Terrace
11. Garage
12. Office
13. Bedroom
14. Bathroom

0 5 10   20ft

WY NATURE CONSERVANCY

Ward | Blake Architects // Tom Ward - Mitch Blake
Lander, wyoming, united states // Photos © Douglas Kahn
www.wardblake.com
Design Architect: Thomas Ward, AIA
Client: Wyoming Chapter of The Nature Conservancy
Client Project Managers: Robert Carter, Ted Zimmerman
Civil Engineer: Joseph Grille, PE

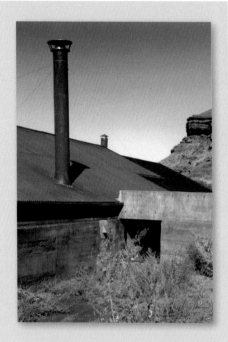

The resource center at Red Canyon Ranch was designed using sustainable technology to capture a "sense of place" and demonstrate energy efficiency.

The site, a gently sloping trailhead leading to the canyon, was chosen for its symbolic expression of the building as a "kiosk" directing visitors to areas of interest.

Rammed earth was used as the primary building material to fulfill the conservancy's desire for low-impact technology, while the custom fabricated steel trusses provide a lightness contrasting the massiveness of the walls.

Water conservation was critical, so a waterless composting toilet system and grey water disposal system were installed.

The rammed earth walls provide thermal mass for even temperature levels, and lighting fixtures utilize compact fluorescent lamping and indirect halogen fixtures to reduce electric consumption and heat load.

El centro de recursos en Red Canyon Ranch fue diseñado utilizando tecnología sostenible para capturar un «sentido de lugar» y demostrar eficiencia energética.

El sitio, un sendero suavemente inclinado que conduce al cañón, fue elegido por su expresión simbólica del edificio como un «kiosco» que dirige a los visitantes a áreas de interés.

Se utilizó tierra apisonada como material de construcción principal para cumplir con el deseo de la conservación de tecnología de bajo impacto, mientras que las cerchas de acero fabricadas a medida proporcionan una ligereza que contrasta con la masividad de las paredes.

La conservación del agua fue crítica, por lo que se instaló un sistema de inodoros composteros sin agua y un sistema de eliminación de aguas grises.

Las paredes de tierra apisonada proporcionan masa térmica para niveles de temperatura uniformes, y las luminarias utilizan lámparas fluorescentes compactas y luminarias halógenas indirectas para reducir el consumo de energía eléctrica y la carga térmica.

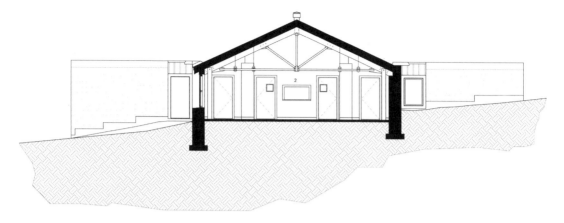

Section

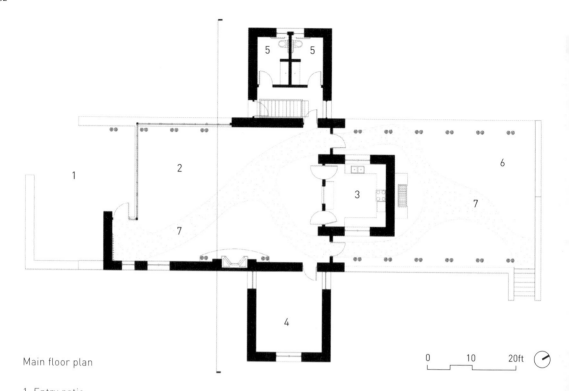

Main floor plan

1. Entry patio
2. Meeting room
3. Kitchen
4. Office
5. Bathroom
6. Outdoor patio
7. Trail

0   10   20ft

WATERSHED STRAWBALE RESIDENCE

Arkin Tilt Architects
Sonoma County, California, United States //
Photos © Edward Caldwell Photography
www.arkintilt.com
Design Architect: David Arkin, AIA
Design Project Manager: Amanda Knowles
Client: Withheld, by owner's request
Drawings by: Arkin Tilt Architects
Structural Engineer: Verdant Structural Engineers
Landscape Architect: Angelica Papio
Civil Engineer: Atterbury & Associates

This off-grid homestead was carefully designed and constructed to minimize impact on the surrounding landscape. The home's indoor/outdoor flow creates a tranquil nature-centered living space for the family.

One of the first projects to use David Easton's compressed earth block (now known as EcoTerra block), the masonry walls deliveries at the remote site provide a warm, textured feel. The upper walls are made of highly-insulating straw bale, covered with lime plaster for thermal mass. Much of the timber used in the home was milled on site, including live-edge slabs used as a guardrail at the stairway to the bedrooms.

The living room roof, planted with vegetation, blends seamlessly with the landscape. Other roofs, made of gently curving corrugated metal, are soften version of typical agrarian structure while mimicing the surrounding tree canopies. Overall, this residence showcases innovative passive solar design with a hybrid palette of sustainable materials.

Este hogar fuera de la red fue cuidadosamente diseñado y construido para minimizar el impacto en el paisaje circundante. El flujo interior/exterior de la casa crea un espacio de vida tranquilo y centrado en la naturaleza para la familia.

Uno de los primeros proyectos en utilizar el bloque de tierra comprimido de David Easton (ahora conocido como bloque EcoTerra), las paredes de mampostería entregadas en el sitio remoto proporcionan una sensación cálida y texturizada. Las paredes superiores están hechas de paja altamente aislante, cubiertas con yeso de cal para la masa térmica. Gran parte de la madera utilizada en la casa se cortó en el sitio, incluidas las losas de borde vivo utilizadas como barandilla en la escalera hacia los dormitorios.

El techo de la sala de estar, plantado con vegetación, se fusiona perfectamente con el paisaje. Otros techos, hechos de láminas corrugadas de metal suavemente curvadas, son una versión más suave de la estructura agraria típica mientras imitan las copas de los árboles circundantes. En general, esta residencia muestra una paleta híbrida de materiales sostenibles e innovadores.

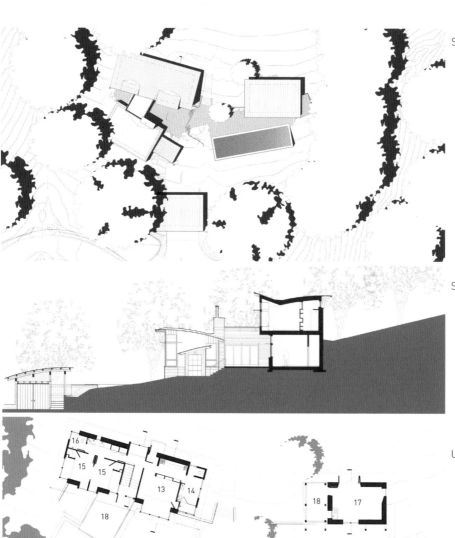

Site and roof plan

Section

Upper level plan

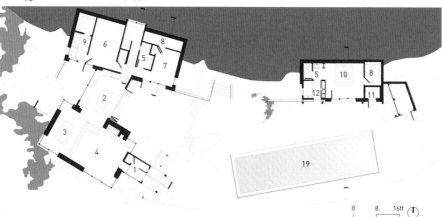

Lower level plan

1. Entry/mudroom
2. Kitchen
3. Dining
4. Living
5. Bathroom
6. Media room
7. Office
8. Storage/mechanical
9. Laundry
10. Pool house
11. Sauna
12. Changing room
13. Master bedroom
14. Master bathroom
15. Kid's bedroom
16. Kid's bathroom
17. Art room
18. Roof deck
19. Pool

0   8   16ft